Verbal Release

AF624486

Inka R

BookLeaf Publishing
India | USA | UK

Presentation by *BookLeaf Publishing*

Web: www.bookleafpub.com

E-mail: info@bookleafpub.com

ISBN: 978-93-5744-492-7

First edition 2022

DEDICATION

To her past, present and future heart.

ACKNOWLEDGEMENT

From a time when little made sense.

Purpose

I swore to myself when I was younger, that if I were to ever stop creating, that I was to stop living. To me, art, music and literature had molded itself into a beating heart in my body and it is the main reason why I continue to breathe today. I'm a broken soul, like many creatives are; constantly trying to run from my own history of unbearable heartaches.
Yes, I struggle with mental health issues; severe anxiety disorder, severe post traumatic stress disorder, severe clinical depression, severe panic disorder and severe hyper-empathy disorder.

When the going gets tough I shut down. Every bone in my body gives up. My brain rewires my world into an impending doom. The faces of those I love turn into the faces of those who have hurt and betrayed me. I spiral and lose faith and trust in everyone around me. Everything collapses into shards from my past and all I have left is my beating heart. A heart that keeps beating because of the depths of creativity it holds. If I didn’t have art, or music, or books - I wouldn’t know where I would be today. It’s morbid, vulnerable but most importantly, true.

You may ask where do my loved ones sit in this equation of gratitude. My family isn't a normal one and I struggle with some of my main personal issues that I’m still trying to overcome and learn from because of my family. I elaborate more in the next chapter. Please bear with me as I'm not used to putting my emotions into words.

It is a constant battle. Tugging and pulling, back and forth, trying to heal while still being hurt.

This small book has the only purpose to document my journey with my mental health over the next month and how this intertwines with impacting my creativity. I aim to expose my personal battles and how it correlates to my art. Some days I may not write in this manner, other days I may write in poems, or short stories.

I chose to do this to remind you reading this that everyone holds pain. Some more than others, but many become guarded and cold-hearted after traumatic events. I am guilty of this. Again, I’m not by any means perfect. But I do know now, after many therapy sessions and support from loved ones, that the bigger I keep my heart and fill it with art and music, the bigger art and music will become prominent in my surroundings to the point where my life support extends from not just my heart but to every single organ and bone in my body. This is my goal. This is my story. I hope my journey is raw, and makes you feel like you are sitting with a friend telling you her struggles and wins.

No More Hiding Will Set Me Free

Today I woke up with the feeling that I was a huge failure. I simply realized that I am a human who is terribly flawed accompanied by a huge mound of trauma. I've lied, I've said hurtful things when I'm upset, and I've put myself into irrational situations. Today, I choose to stop hiding behind such unrealistic representations of myself and live each moment as honestly and mindfully as I can. I can accept that at times I can be stubborn, and silly - and for that, I am sorry to those who I have hurt.

At the same time, I would once again like to thank those who have also hurt me. Because without you I wouldn't have realized my own flaws, and sometimes it takes the worst in others to bring out the worst in me. For me to see. In light and very clearly. The truth of who I am.

I am not only intelligent, loving, kind-hearted, generous, beautiful and loyal but I am also sensitive, insecure, guilty, self-critical and can feel absolutely worthless at times.

These harsher realities which I'm currently facing are difficult to digest - as I have always seen myself as a positive person who constantly bends backwards for those that I love. But recently I have learnt that I am also a contributor to issues in my relationships because of my obscured understandings of my depression.

I am fighting every day with mental illnesses, yes… but everyone around me is also fighting their own battles. Everyone has shit. I can't sit here and continue to dwell and feed into an idealization of my illnesses. I must accept. Process. Forgive. And move on. This is the growth that I need. I need to learn a lesson about honesty and how incredibly important my words can be. However, I'm sure you know, trying to grow from grief isn't an easy stead and the time in which it takes to process grief can take years. The idea that I will be hurt by yet another person while still trying to heal from the past is incredibly daunting. The grieving process of anything isn't pretty - and does hurt like hell.

Here is my truth. I am scared that I won't be able to handle heartache on heartache as I try to process past traumatic events simultaneously. That takes strength and support, yet I feel isolated and drained.

(Please note - I have beautiful friends, and family as a support system but I developed avoidance issues from childhood traumas as I experience a lack of a motherly figure in crucial parts of my life. As well as a development of abandonment issues from this and losing quite a lot of important figures I looked up to in my family growing up. Therefore, I have a bad habit of isolating myself when I am hurting, as I'm scared of being vulnerable. Kinda trying to work on that by writing this book.)

How does this correlate to my art?

I sometimes feel like I hide behind my paintings as art can be so subjective and open for interpretation, it makes me feel like I don't have to explain the true meaning of an artwork. I can use the excuse of 'it can mean whatever you want it to mean to you'. Which is also true, however that's just me using my adapted avoidance issues I was talking about earlier to not have to converse about the states of my mental health and how it is represented in my art. My works always derive from emotion -

always. I tend to express my struggles and inner pains because I'm not the best at communicating my past and feelings verbally. (If you haven't gathered that already.) Ever since I was young and beginning to develop these 'survival tactics', I always turned to creativity. I was always drawing, writing, dancing (I was a cheerleader and a ballet dancer… wild.), acting, performing in festivals, plays, and musicals. I became very independent very young, as I moved schools every six to twelve months and was never able to keep a friend. (Note, another reason why I have abandonment issues, and struggle to open up to new people on a deeper level).

Any form of art became a coping mechanism for me. It became my safe place where I could be true to who I was and never had to explain myself to anyone. It was perfect (it still is). But now that I'm an adult, art isn't as easy as putting a brush to a canvas anymore. There's a process. My mind has grown a lot since my childhood of course, and now themes of 'sadness' aren't just 'I feel sad so I will paint something sad'. For me, sadness now entails traumatic and triggering events which are difficult to process and that combined with avoidance issues means putting my paint to a canvas is me 'facing my trauma's'. This is terrifying.

Please don’t mistake my fears for a lack of love for it though - because it still does provide me an escape to become free of things holding me back that I can't necessarily articulate. It’s just much more of an emotional and complex process compared to when I was five and didn’t have anything to worry about apart from my own feelings.

Vapor

I arose this morning with heavy vapor in my
lungs,
Struggling to breathe with fears of the things
that I've done.
Nothing could calm me except for the floods of
my tears,
Repairing the drought of a strong woman
underneath.
I fight to get up, find my feet, see my hands,
Trembling, I grab my phone to text my therapist
for a plan.
In seconds the aid was flying in,
Beginning to breathe and realize it was my
depression.
I separate my emotions from the practicalities of
the day,
To understand, I am struggling with too much on
my plate.
Not because of what my demons had to say,
I thanked them very much, got up, and wished
them a nice day.

Future

My art has been betrothed to the grave today as I step foot outside of my delusions and face such a sad and dystopian reality. No time to draw, read or sing to my heart's content as I am abiding by the systematic society in which I live in. I must work, study, and get vaccinated. (Well they are all choices I have the freedom of abiding to or not, but if I became ignorant to these things, my chance of surviving this world is quite slim).

For study, I am doing a Bachelor of Fine Arts (aiming to do a PHD) at the Queensland College of Arts (sounds so unnecessarily prestigious) however I focus directly on arts history. At the moment, of course, I am learning about the westerners art history with portraiture which juxtaposes to the other courses I'm doing which is analyzing artworks from Aboriginal and Indigenous peoples in relation to assimilation and genocide.

Recently I was painting a large skeleton hand mural at a local cafe, to which I came to the epiphany that I am a Thai woman who knows barely anything about her country's history -

specifically art history. I soon came to find out after some research, that Thailand's history isn't taught in schools and is usually common knowledge by story telling passed down to each generation. I personally haven't been told these stories as my family elders have all passed, and the time in which I was meant to learn - Covid restrictions disabled me from spending time with them before their passing. I further researched 'Thai Art History' and to my dismay, yet again, an enormous lack of research. Which is quite baffling to me as I've grown up seeing many stories told through the traditional paintings in temples - and there is no lack of it. In fact there's, over 40,000 temples in Thailand yet there is such a shortage of research which goes into the traditions and meanings of each story. So that was the moment I discovered my life long relationship commitment. I've always known I wanted to complete a PHD, and I did have an idea prior to this in what my thesis would be about, but this is what I have decided to do now. I want to be able to begin research of my own traditions and explore the vast unknown. There is so much to learn that I don't think I will be able to capture even the essence of richness in which Thai Art History has to offer - because even the knowledge I have now is what I thought to be fairly extensive.

Alongside current courses offered in art history studies - I hope to one day provide a space in which I can share the stories of my cultures too.

Anyways, that's all I have for today - considering I didn't quite have the chance to be creative, I thought I'd share a recent moment when I had an incredibly creative idea.

Ex Lover

Not another wimp could recover from within,
My structures became numb and succumbed to
illness,
Both mental and physical today my wars
represented,
With just me at the front lines, with not one
helping hand.

Isolation in this moment feels incredibly close,
Yet loved ones close by seem so far away from
me the most.

I had a dear friend rise up from my past,
With confusing messages, talking about how our
past love still makes a mark.
He was one that I loved and one that hurt me the
most.
The details don't matter now, as this past has
become a ghost.
I'm sorry my friend, for losing touch over the
years,
But I've paved my own path without you and
right now I love happily.
I hope you are well, and all is forgiven,

I still love you too, just not in the same way you were wishing.
I know that our paths will cross over soon,
And I hope by then we can laugh about how dumb we were to the moon.
I hope you are safe, in Paris, with your new lover,
Maybe bring her back home, I'm sure we'd have much to banter.

Sake

A realization bestowed itself so childishly onto me today as I was beginning my day at work, I completely forgot, that as an adult… a working adult, I have money.

I was overhearing the ladies in my workplace boast about the expensive dinners they have organized with their families, lovers and friends as they frolic around in new potential gowns for the night. Constantly replying to the ladies "You are so lucky, I wish I was going to a fancy dinner tonight."

Just to realize there is absolutely nothing stopping me but myself. I have the money, I have the dress, I have a lover, I have friends, and I had the perfect expensive joint in mind.

Badabing, Badaboom - all of the sudden I was going on a double date, with people I love and to eat some food that I wanted to make love to. Spicy.

The slip dress slid on like melted butter on a corn cob,

The heels sparkled and strutted in the rhythm of a Buddy Guy song.
The sky darkened and the boys and girls were getting ready for a dance.
Silence was shared which spoke louder than any word, on how damn good the food was.
A priceless joy, the silence in which good food brings.
Smiles with teeth holding back the half chewed food occasionally appeared,
The confusion of how to behave in such an expensive place was exchanged through side eyes from across the tables.
Giggles in between every sake shot, and cheering on each other to complete the longest eating marathon possible.
The 'holy shit' moment when the final bill came close to $500.
The 'oh well we've done it now so let's keep going' moment after,
Leading us to an arcade where we battled it out in games like mario kart and hoops,
A dress was broken, champions were crowned, and slinkies were won.
Finally, the moment came where the lovers were tired out and needed to be tucked away.
The bodies flew onto their beds, exhausted, full, grateful and happy, The lights went out, and the rest may remain a mystery.

Sleeping Shadows

Familiarity of a happier parallel showed itself in a gentle way,
Through the eyes of strangers, through the smiles of loved ones,
Within the drumming of a song and in the scent of the rain.
I became overwhelmed with laughter to the point where it ate me whole.
My cheeks were marked with a reminiscence from a story that made me so.
Simultaneously there was a shadow pressing against my back, trying to let itself in,
To infest my mind and turn all of it into a grim sin.

I sung it a song, that came from the tongues of my lands,
It lulled the shadow back to sleep, into the palm of my hands.
I held it gently, with my voice softening.
I thank it, for making me strong,
And sorry, forever treating it so wrong.
I close my hands into a fist, as it's deep into a snore,
I opened them back up again, and it was gone.

Treasure Man

Beginning the day with a bounce and a dance,
Running down to the antique store in hopes to
find a treasured man.
I came across one that charmed me in, running
his fingers down my leg,
Losing track of what he was whispering.
A salesman who emerges only when I think I
need him,
He lives within me, with a cheeky little grin.
I found a treasure, that my treasure man liked,
It was simple, domestic and nothing much of a
delight,
Yet the treasure man whispered to me that my
need for it is un-doubtful,
So the simple thing came home with me,
And the treasure man went back to sleep feeling
bountiful.

The simple thing was needy,
Demanding more space than I had to give,
Burdening me harshly as I try to fit it in.
As the hours went by a realization dawned upon
me,

The treasure man told me a lie on what he thought I needed,
This simple thing wasn't giving me any purpose,
In fact it began to cause me to bleed and ache in pain from forcing it.
I learnt a simple lesson from this simple thing,
Don't always listen to what the treasure man tries to sing.

Wish

Overwhelmed with a burden of self-criticism,
I walk outside to sit by the crickets at night and listen.
My fingers roll a cigarette and my ears are suddenly filled with old ballads from times of when I was younger.
I look up, and see a moon, so full and bright it lit up the entire park in front of me.
I begin to zone into the music and flow with the moon.
As I dance on my own to my own rhythms, I watch a plane slowly drift across the night sky below the stars and I begin to imagine where it may be traveling.
I stopped and stood watching this plane, fly from one edge of the sky to the other,
And then suddenly, almost miraculously,
A shooting star soared through the sky in the opposite direction of the plane and gave me a few seconds to think of a wish.
Overwhelmed by all the happenings I could only think of one thing,
I wished a wish that might not be worth telling,

As the elders before us have said, once a wish is
told the wishes life will end,
So I will leave you with your imagination, and
what you might have wished for in this moment
instead.

Womanhood

That time has rolled around again,
when my womanhood is pressuring my health
and calls for a reset.
I lose energy, I become overcome with emotions
and I begin to cry, questioning why did the gods
choose to create me like this?
The power of a woman can rule the universes if
she wished,
She is gifted with the knowledge of wielding
anything if she wants it.
She has the power to create life from nothing,
and the ability to end a life without killing it.
She can do pretty much anything, except maybe
grow a beard.
I realize that I was born a woman in this life
because I am capable of ruling my universe,
however I wish to.
At the small cost of blood and pain.
Tiredness, and vulnerability.
These things are worth the sacrifice of being a
woman.
Because the moment I accepted my powers I
was given,
I became a force that should never be reckoned
with.

Lithium Toads

Once again the blistering toads have emerged
and made their presence seen,
They croaked so loudly with puss oozing out of
their skin,
Poisoning the souls of whoever dared to touch
them,
Opening up old wounds,and infesting with
various lithiums.

A dawning fear ate my corpse up whole,
As I realize these toads are starting to appear on
my road.
I was cramming responsibilities into the cracks
of my heart,
Trying to fill the broken bricks which was
caused from a painning past.
Unfortunately distractions only run their course
for so long,
As the cracks reappear as each task is
performed.

The toads kept coming, in their armies and their
fleets.
As I stand here alone, with only myself and
broken bricks.

Moving in closer, they sway and grow larger,
And before I knew it they were so close I had no escape from danger.

I stood there surrendering, with only myself and broken bricks,
Showing my naked truth, and daring the toads to have a feast.

They became shocked at my strength, and fearlessness of them,
They tried to poison me again and again with all of their lithiums.
I stood there offering myself, do as you wish,
As I couldn't run away with the weight of those bricks.
They tried to hurt me, over and over again,
Only to realize they can't hurt a soul who was already broken.
All of their poisons were exhausted by the end, and they turned back into young frogs, who were innocent and not a foe but a friend.
I stood there and let them give their poisons to me, Because through releasing their pains, at least they will become free.
They hopped off my road and went on with their lives, As I still stand with bricks broken, wondering how I will try fixing them this time.

Blood Art

As I hang my truth up on walls in colors,
The sounds of hammers and nails weren't as
loud as my heart shuddered.
I realize my guts were bleeding down the walls
of this space,
Never intending for such things to be seen by
your face.
I reach up high, as I embellish my pain,
Trying to create beauty out of so much dismay.
If one did not know me they would see colors of
life,
But those that do know I paint freely from a
troubled mind.

Masks

A disappointment can turn so ugly,
When your loved ones aren't there when you need them so desperately.
Riddled with anxieties for days before a show,
Not keeping down a single meal, and my body was running low.
My heart was cut open, and bled out onto these canvases,
Only to be left feeling empty, wondering why did I choose to do this?
I guess I wanted someone out there to not feel alone,
The others who bleed like me, draining their hearts trying to find hope.

It was an interesting night, as some roles were reversed.
My paintings usually hide behind me, as I protect them with the charm of my words.
Yet on this night, everything was different,
I hid behind my paintings, letting them speak for me as I felt nothing was left.
I was hiding so much, behind the smiles from the compliments,

No one knew that I felt like I was dealing with
so much sadness.
It was a success, for an artist who connected
with her admirers,
And for that I am grateful, because if it wasn't, I
would have struggled to hold the burdens of
what came next.

The night moved on, as I still lived in the past.
Wanting so desperately to be happy, however
nothing but hurt could be seen from my mask.
I tried, I really tried, to be proud of what I did,
But it's that feeling of disappointment that
couldn't bring me to it.

Family

I called my family as I fell and had no strength to get up.
I got kicked to the dirt in more ways than one.
I left my second home as a mess, such a mess.
And arrived at my family home, to a house that was well kept.
Welcomed by Mr Gingy, my beautiful cat,
All of the sudden I could breathe, I can't remember the last time I did that.
My old bed was soft, with french sheets and silk cloth.
My old garden was wild, filled with weeds and veggie stalks.
My little brother remained the same, to himself, not by me,
My father was caring, I knew he was worrying, always thinking how is she?
He cooked my favorite foods and told jokes that we two would get,
Watched doco's on his rockstars until it was time for us to sleep.
It feels good to be home,
It feels good to breathe.
Thank god or whomever I have to, that I have my family.

Someone Like Me

A rest has been overlooked for many times
before now,
Not recognizing how fast time can be lost, when
you fall asleep at your bow.
I couldn't get up, as I sunk so low into my
sheets,
The feeling of being home lets my body be at
ease.
I spent the day resting, my heart, my mind, and
my body.
It felt so unfamiliar, to be doing absolutely
nothing.
For a woman who takes on so much that her
own plate is always cracking,
Trying to balance the pieces in her hands, under
mountains of stress with not enough healing.
Why do I take on so much more than I can hold?
It's because I feel the need to fix and hold up
everyone else,
As that's something I don't have for myself.
I want others to know what it's like to have me,
A person who will do anything, take a bullet for
you if need be. I wish I had someone who in that
sense was like me, For if I had a me holding me,
it would be much easier to be.

Good, Good, Good

Honesty with yourself is a prime example of a blessing in disguise.
At first it wears a mask that's so daunting and seems hard to untie.
The truth is always hard when it's for realized flaws.
As you look into the eyes of one truth, all of the sudden there is more.
Even though this is called growth, and it should definitely be celebrated,
God damn it is hard to accept and try to learn from your mistakes.
It's good, I'm good, but not as perfect as I would like to be,
But I've come to the realization that no one is seen as perfect as they themselves wish to see.
Learning to be kind to myself, and allowing myself make mistakes,
So I can learn more about myself and others and how to be better.
I'm coming to terms with the fact that people love people,
But people also have the power to hurt each other.

And learning how can I hold space and give
opportunities for others when they do hurt me,
So they can grow and be better for themselves,
others and I.
Lessons on lessons on lessons, always,always,
always.
It’s good, good, good.

Granny

The gods molded a soul too beautiful,
This world is undeserving of her grace.
She can heal one's heart, through the power of her smile.
She can stun a room, without effort.
This woman is the epiphany of beauty, she lives among the other angels who sing the same hymns only angels this beautiful do.

A Poem For You

The projection of emotion through mere words
is a powerful tool,
It can destroy cities and it could end wars with
peace treaties.
Words can send a soul too broken off a bridge,
Or they could lift that broken one up, with
strength to keep fighting, again.
I give you my words to show vulnerability.
I give you my words willingly, lovingly,
generously.
Your eyes that are mine right now, please read
what's next openly.

Days can be as dark as nights and nights as cold
as the snow.
Your heart can become empty, and you may at
times lose your soul.
This is necessary, this needs to happen.
Without knowing yourself through such a
burden, you won't know yourself un-saddened.
You must breathe gently through the cracks of
toppling bricks upon you,
Slowly, embracingly, gratefully.
And emerge among the piles of the weight
oneday, so you may truly be free.

Bye For Now

My beautiful home, I am about to depart.
The trees sing me a song, wishing me well for my crafts.
The wind kisses my face as it knows it will be missed,
There's nothing like the cold breeze from the mountains in which I live.
The mulberry trees hope that I will return soon,
For it will bare me with more fruits for me to make inks for my muse.
My cat, Mr Gingy, is shy and clueless,
He keeps demanding for scratches, unknowingly demanding for a time that is becoming very precious.
The concept of time here is nothing short but of non-existent,
As each time I come back, nothing changes, it remains consistent.
I will be back soon for when the city is too much,
You will be missed, I hope you stay well with a sprinkle of luck.

Me, Is All I Need

Through you, I have found an incredible amount
of pain.
Through us, I have found an unapologetic
healing.
Through me, I found strength and love.
Through her I found betrayal.
Through him I found toxicity.
Through time, I found that I am all I need.

A Dance With Demons

I anticipated clouds threaded with golden silks,
It hoped for storms and thunder from the unholy powers.
I dreamt of drinks which bubbled joyously underneath the lioness above,
It imagined fires which swept through bone to bone, an unbearable pain emerging from what was evil within.
I listened to songs that lured my soul around the fingers of passion, love and you,
While it played songs that tried to call up the viscous sirens from deep within the sea and take whichever thing it ever pleased.
I live with it, but it does not live with me.
I see it, it is there, but I bend my back into pieces to never let it free.
It awaits in the shadows constantly,
I like to keep it there, never within me, or beside me.

www.ingramcontent.com/pod-product-compliance
Lightning Source LLC
Chambersburg PA
CBHW051747130826
49812CB00033B/1032
9789357444927